# MY GARDEN

By Sarah Keane • Illustrated by Bettina Guthridge

HOUGHTON MIFFLIN COMPANY
BOSTON
ATLANTA DALLAS GENEVA, ILLINOIS PALO ALTO PRINCETON

In my garden I use

a watering can, a small fork, and a trowel for digging.

In my garden I like to

plant seedlings,

water the flowers, and sweep up the leaves.

In my garden I wear

a hat to keep the sun off, gloves to keep my hands clean,

and old clothes to get dirty in.

In my garden I find

spiders and worms,

butterflies and bees,

and sometimes a frog.

In my garden I see

flowers and trees,

vegetables and herbs, and the goldfish in the pond.

In my garden I have

a favorite seat for reading, a big tree for climbing, and a swing for singing.

In my garden I know

a shady spot for picnics, a noisy place to play,

and a secret space for hiding.

My garden is a very special place.